Public Worship
with
Communion by Extension

C000002175

Church House Publishing

Published by   Church House Publishing
                Church House
                Great Smith Street
                London SW1P 3NZ

Copyright ©   *The Archbishops' Council 2001*

                First published 2001

                0 7151 2053 0

Printed and bound by ArklePrint Ltd, Northampton
on 80 gsm Dutchman Ivory

Typeset in 9 on 12 point Gill Sans
by John Morgan and Shirley Thompson/Omnific
Designed by Derek Birdsall RDI

Contents

Notes

¶ *Public Worship with Communion by Extension*

1. Explicit permission must be obtained from the bishop for the use of this rite. This permission should relate to specific pastoral circumstances, thus emphasizing the exceptional nature of this ministry. See also the Guidelines issued by the House of Bishops on pages 32–33.

2. In parishes or cures in which Public Worship with Communion by Extension has been authorized, care should be taken to ensure that a Sunday celebration of Holy Communion continues to take place regularly in each church. Public Worship with Communion by Extension will normally take place on Sundays and Principal Holy Days. Exceptionally, the rite may be appropriate on other occasions.

3. This service is led only by a person specifically authorized by the bishop; this may be a deacon, Reader or other lay person who has received appropriate training. Those who have permission under Canon B 12 may share in the giving of communion.

4. If the minister is a deacon, Reader or lay worker authorized under Canon E 7, the appropriate vesture is worn.

5. Care should be taken to ensure that those who play any part in the administration of Communion by Extension treat the elements in a seemly and dignified manner and observe the rubrics in the rite provided.

6. Proper provision must be made for the consecrated bread and wine to be brought to the church from the celebration of Holy Communion in a seemly and dignified manner. They should be placed upon the Holy Table and covered with a clean white cloth.

7. Proper care should be taken to ensure as far as possible that the consecrated elements are adequate to meet the needs of the congregation. If the bread and wine prove insufficient for the number of communicants, there can be no supplementary consecration in the course of this service.

¶ General Notes

¶ Preparation

Careful devotional preparation before the service is recommended for every communicant. A Form of Preparation for public or private use is provided (page 35).

¶ Communicant members of other Churches

Baptized persons who are communicant members of other Churches which subscribe to the doctrine of the Holy Trinity and are in good standing in their own Church shall be admitted to Communion in accordance with Canon B 15A.

The following Notes to the Order for the Celebration of Holy Communion in *Common Worship: Services and Prayers for the Church of England* (pages 330–335) also apply to Order One: 1–16, 19, 21, 22.

For General Rules for Regulating Authorized Forms of Service, see page 40.

Order One

¶ *The Gathering*

At the entry of the minister a hymn may be sung.

The minister may say

In the name of the Father,
and of the Son,
and of the Holy Spirit.

All **Amen.**

The Greeting

The minister welcomes the people using these or other appropriate words

The Lord be with you

All **and also with you.**

(or)

Grace, mercy and peace
from God our Father
and the Lord Jesus Christ
be with you

All **and also with you.**

From Easter Day to Pentecost, this acclamation follows

Alleluia. Christ is risen.

All **He is risen indeed. Alleluia.**

Words of welcome or introduction may be said.

Brothers and sisters, in the Gospel of Saint Luke we read:

> At supper with his disciples on the night he was betrayed Jesus
> took a cup, and after giving thanks he said, 'Take this and divide
> it among yourselves; for I tell you that from now on I will not
> drink of the fruit of the vine until the kingdom of God comes.'
> Then he took a loaf of bread, and when he had given thanks, he
> broke it and gave it to them, saying, 'This is my body, which is
> given for you. Do this in remembrance of me.'

We have come together in our Father's presence to offer him praise
and thanksgiving, to hear and receive his holy Word, to bring before
him the needs of the world and to ask his forgiveness of our sins.
In union with those who celebrate [have celebrated] the Eucharist
at *N*… this day, we seek God's grace in Holy Communion. For as
often as we eat this bread and drink the cup in obedience to his
command, we proclaim the Lord's death until he comes.

Prayer of Preparation

This prayer may be said

All **Almighty God,**
to whom all hearts are open,
all desires known,
and from whom no secrets are hidden:
cleanse the thoughts of our hearts
by the inspiration of your Holy Spirit,
that we may perfectly love you,
and worthily magnify your holy name;
through Christ our Lord.
Amen.

Prayers of Penitence

The Summary of the Law, the Commandments, the Beatitudes or the Comfortable Words may be used.

A minister uses a seasonal invitation to confession or these or other suitable words

God so loved the world
that he gave his only Son Jesus Christ
to save us from our sins,
to be our advocate in heaven,
and to bring us to eternal life.

Let us confess our sins in penitence and faith,
firmly resolved to keep God's commandments
and to live in love and peace with all.

All **Almighty God, our heavenly Father,**
we have sinned against you
and against our neighbour
in thought and word and deed,
through negligence, through weakness,
through our own deliberate fault.
We are truly sorry
and repent of all our sins.
For the sake of your Son Jesus Christ,
who died for us,
forgive us all that is past
and grant that we may serve you in newness of life
to the glory of your name.
Amen.

(or)

All **Most merciful God,**
Father of our Lord Jesus Christ,
we confess that we have sinned
in thought, word and deed.
We have not loved you with our whole heart.
We have not loved our neighbours as ourselves.
In your mercy
forgive what we have been,
help us to amend what we are,
and direct what we shall be;
that we may do justly,
love mercy,
and walk humbly with you, our God.
Amen.

Or, with suitable penitential sentences, the Kyrie eleison may be used

Lord, have mercy.
All **Lord, have mercy.**

Christ, have mercy.
All **Christ, have mercy.**

Lord, have mercy.
All **Lord, have mercy.**

If another confession has already been used, the Kyrie eleison may be
used without interpolation here or after the prayer for absolution.

The minister says

May almighty God,
who forgives all who truly repent,
have mercy upon us,
pardon and deliver us from all our sins,
confirm and strengthen us in all goodness,
and keep us in life eternal;
through Jesus Christ our Lord.
All **Amen.**

Gloria in Excelsis

The Gloria in excelsis may be used.

All **Glory to God in the highest,**
and peace to his people on earth.

Lord God, heavenly King,
almighty God and Father,
we worship you, we give you thanks,
we praise you for your glory.

Lord Jesus Christ, only Son of the Father,
Lord God, Lamb of God,
you take away the sin of the world:
have mercy on us;
you are seated at the right hand of the Father:
receive our prayer.

For you alone are the Holy One,
you alone are the Lord,
you alone are the Most High, Jesus Christ,
with the Holy Spirit,
in the glory of God the Father.
Amen.

The Collect

The minister introduces a period of silent prayer with the words
'Let us pray' or a more specific bidding.

The Collect is said, and all respond

All **Amen.**

¶ The Liturgy of the Word

Readings

The readings are governed by authorized lectionary provision.

Either one or two readings from Scripture precede the Gospel reading.

At the end of each the reader may say

This is the word of the Lord.

All **Thanks be to God.**

The psalm or canticle follows the first reading; other hymns and songs may be used between the readings.

Gospel Reading

An acclamation may herald the Gospel reading.

When the Gospel is announced the reader says

Hear the Gospel of our Lord Jesus Christ according to *N.*

All **Glory to you, O Lord.**

At the end

This is the Gospel of the Lord.

All **Praise to you, O Christ.**

Sermon

The Creed

On Sundays and Principal Holy Days an authorized translation of the Nicene Creed is used, or on occasion the Apostles' Creed or an authorized Affirmation of Faith may be used (see pages 138–148 in Common Worship: Services and Prayers for the Church of England).

All **We believe in one God,
the Father, the Almighty,
maker of heaven and earth,
of all that is,
seen and unseen.**

**We believe in one Lord, Jesus Christ,
the only Son of God,
eternally begotten of the Father,
God from God, Light from Light,
true God from true God,
begotten, not made,
of one Being with the Father;
through him all things were made.
For us and for our salvation he came down from heaven,
was incarnate from the Holy Spirit and the Virgin Mary
and was made man.
For our sake he was crucified under Pontius Pilate;
he suffered death and was buried.
On the third day he rose again
in accordance with the Scriptures;
he ascended into heaven
and is seated at the right hand of the Father.
He will come again in glory to judge the living and the dead,
and his kingdom will have no end.**

**We believe in the Holy Spirit,
the Lord, the giver of life,
who proceeds from the Father and the Son,
who with the Father and the Son is worshipped and glorified,
who has spoken through the prophets.
We believe in one holy catholic and apostolic Church.
We acknowledge one baptism for the forgiveness of sins.
We look for the resurrection of the dead,
and the life of the world to come.
Amen.**

Prayers of Intercession and Thanksgiving

One of the forms on pages 281–289 in Common Worship: Services and Prayers for the Church of England *or other suitable words may be used.*

The prayers usually include these concerns and may follow this sequence:

¶   *The Church of Christ*

¶   *Creation, human society, the Sovereign and those in authority*

¶   *The local community*

¶   *Those who suffer*

¶   *The communion of saints*

Thanksgiving and praise may be offered for the great acts of God in creation and redemption.

These responses may be used

Lord, in your mercy
All   **hear our prayer.**

(or)

Lord, hear us.
All   **Lord, graciously hear us.**

And at the end

Merciful Father,
All   **accept these prayers**
for the sake of your Son,
our Saviour Jesus Christ.
Amen.

¶ The Liturgy of the Sacrament

The Peace

The minister may introduce the Peace thus

In fellowship with the whole Church of God, with all who have been brought together by the Holy Spirit to worship on this day, and particularly with our brothers and sisters at *N* … who have celebrated the Eucharist, let us rejoice that we are called to be part of the body of Christ.

All **Though we are many, we are one body,
because we all share in one bread.**

or a seasonal sentence (pages 290 and 300–329 in Common Worship: Services and Prayers for the Church of England) *may be used.*

The minister then says

The peace of the Lord be always with you.

All **And also with you.**

These words may be added
Let us offer one another a sign of peace.

All may exchange a sign of peace.

A hymn may be sung.

Pre- Church Militant

Actonel
(risedronate sodium tablets)

Libya
Afghanistan
Famine in Horn of Africa.

Charlotte Jordan
Rosemary

e his life.

of bread.

ue drink.

he Lamb.

he cross.

You strengthen us with your Spirit,
the new wine of your Kingdom.
In Christ you are food for the hungry,
refreshment for the weary.
Blessed are you, our Creator and Redeemer.
Blessed be God for ever.

The Lord's Prayer

As our Saviour taught us, so we pray

All   **Our Father in heaven,**
hallowed be your name,
your kingdom come,
your will be done,
on earth as in heaven.
Give us today our daily bread.
Forgive us our sins
as we forgive those who sin against us.
Lead us not into temptation
but deliver us from evil.
For the kingdom, the power,
and the glory are yours
now and for ever.
Amen.

(or)

Let us pray with confidence as our Saviour has taught us

All   **Our Father, who art in heaven,**
hallowed be thy name;
thy kingdom come;
thy will be done;
on earth as it is in heaven.
Give us this day our daily bread.
And forgive us our trespasses,
as we forgive those who trespass against us.
And lead us not into temptation;
but deliver us from evil.
For thine is the kingdom,
the power and the glory,
for ever and ever.
Amen.

Giving of Communion

The minister moves to the Holy Table and says

The Church of God, of which we are members, has taken bread and wine and given thanks over them according to our Lord's command. These holy gifts have been brought to us that we too may share in the communion of the body and blood of Christ.

Silence is kept.

The minister says

Draw near with faith.
Receive the body of our Lord Jesus Christ
which he gave for you
and his blood which he shed for you.
Eat and drink
in remembrance that he died for you,
and feed on him in your hearts
by faith with thanksgiving.

(or)

Jesus is the Lamb of God
who takes away the sin of the world.
Blessed are those who are called to his supper.

All **Lord, I am not worthy to receive you,
but only say the word, and I shall be healed.**

(or)

God's holy gifts
for God's holy people.

All **Jesus Christ is holy,
Jesus Christ is Lord,
to the glory of God the Father.**

or, from Easter Day to Pentecost

Alleluia. Christ our passover is sacrificed for us.

All **Therefore let us keep the feast. Alleluia.**

All **We do not presume
to come to this your table, merciful Lord,
trusting in our own righteousness,
but in your manifold and great mercies.
We are not worthy
so much as to gather up the crumbs under your table.
But you are the same Lord
whose nature is always to have mercy.
Grant us therefore, gracious Lord,
so to eat the flesh of your dear Son Jesus Christ
and to drink his blood,
that our sinful bodies may be made clean by his body
and our souls washed through his most precious blood,
and that we may evermore dwell in him, and he in us.
Amen.**

(or)

All **Most merciful Lord,
your love compels us to come in.
Our hands were unclean,
our hearts were unprepared;
we were not fit
even to eat the crumbs from under your table.
But you, Lord, are the God of our salvation,
and share your bread with sinners.
So cleanse and feed us
with the precious body and blood of your Son,
that he may live in us and we in him;
and that we, with the whole company of Christ,
may sit and eat in your kingdom.
Amen.**

The minister and people receive communion.

Authorized words of distribution are used and the communicant replies
Amen.

During the distribution hymns and anthems may be sung.

*Any consecrated bread and wine which is not required for purposes
of communion is consumed at the end of the distribution or after
the service.*

Prayer after Communion

Silence is kept.

The Post Communion or another suitable prayer is said.

All may say one of these prayers

All **Almighty God,**
we thank you for feeding us
with the body and blood of your Son Jesus Christ.
Through him we offer you our souls and bodies
to be a living sacrifice.
Send us out
in the power of your Spirit
to live and work
to your praise and glory.
Amen.

(or)

All **Father of all,**
we give you thanks and praise,
that when we were still far off
you met us in your Son and brought us home.
Dying and living, he declared your love,
gave us grace, and opened the gate of glory.
May we who share Christ's body live his risen life;
we who drink his cup bring life to others;
we whom the Spirit lights give light to the world.
Keep us firm in the hope you have set before us,
so we and all your children shall be free,
and the whole earth live to praise your name;
through Christ our Lord.
Amen.

¶ The Dismissal

A hymn may be sung.

All **The grace of our Lord Jesus Christ,
and the love of God,
and the fellowship of the Holy Spirit
be with us all evermore.
Amen.**

A minister says

Go in peace to love and serve the Lord.
All **In the name of Christ. Amen.**

(or)

Go in the peace of Christ.
All **Thanks be to God.**

or, from Easter Day to Pentecost

Go in the peace of Christ. Alleluia, alleluia.
All **Thanks be to God. Alleluia, alleluia.**

Other suitable words of dismissal may be used.

The minister and people depart.

Notes

For Notes to Public Worship with Communion by Extension,
see page v.

¶ *General Notes*

¶ Preparation

Careful devotional preparation before the service is recommended
for every communicant. A Form of Preparation for public or private
use is provided (page 35).

¶ Communicant members of other Churches

Baptized persons who are communicant members of other
Churches which subscribe to the doctrine of the Holy Trinity
and are in good standing in their own Church shall be admitted
to Communion in accordance with Canon B 15A.

The following Notes to the Order for the Celebration of Holy
Communion in *Common Worship: Services and Prayers for the Church
of England* (pages 330–335) also apply to Order Two: 1–16, 19, 21,
22, 24–26, 29.

For General Rules for Regulating Authorized Forms of Service,
see page 40.

Order Two

At the entry of the minister a hymn may be sung.

The minister says

Dearly beloved, in the Gospel of Saint Luke we read: 'When the hour was come, Jesus sat down, and the twelve apostles with him. And he said unto them, With desire I have desired to eat this passover with you before I suffer: For I say unto you, I will not any more eat therof, until it be fulfilled in the kingdom of God. And he took the cup, and gave thanks, and said, Take this and divide it among yourselves: for I say unto you, I will not drink of the fruit of the vine, until the kingdom of God come. And he took bread, and gave thanks, and brake it, and gave unto them, saying, This is my body which is given for you: do this in remembrance of me.'

We are assembled and met together to render thanks for the great benefits that we have received at the hands of Almighty God, to set forth his most worthy praise, to hear his most holy Word, to acknowledge and confess our manifold sins and wickedness, to ask those things which are requisite and necessary, as well for the body as the soul, and, in union with those who celebrate [have celebrated] the Holy Communion at N… this day, to partake of the spiritual food of the most precious Body and Blood of Christ in remembrance of his death and resurrection. For as often as we eat this bread and drink this cup in obedience to his command, we proclaim the Lord's death until he comes.

Prayer of Preparation

Almighty God,
unto whom all hearts be open,
all desires known,
and from whom no secrets are hid:
cleanse the thoughts of our hearts
by the inspiration of thy Holy Spirit,
that we may perfectly love thee,
and worthily magnify thy holy name;
through Christ our Lord.

All **Amen.**

The Commandments

*The minister reads the Ten Commandments and the people make
the response. Or, except on the first Sundays of Advent and Lent,
the Summary of the Law or Kyrie eleison may be used.*

God spake these words and said:
I am the Lord thy God; thou shalt have none other gods but me.

All **Lord, have mercy upon us,
and incline our hearts to keep this law.**

Thou shalt not make to thyself any graven image,
nor the likeness of any thing that is in heaven above,
or in the earth beneath, or in the water under the earth.
Thou shalt not bow down to them, nor worship them:
for I the Lord thy God am a jealous God,
and visit the sins of the fathers upon the children
    unto the third and fourth generation of them that hate me,
and shew mercy unto thousands in them that love me
    and keep my commandments.

All **Lord, have mercy upon us,
and incline our hearts to keep this law.**

Thou shalt not take the name of the Lord thy God in vain:
for the Lord will not hold him guiltless that taketh his name in vain.

All **Lord, have mercy upon us,
and incline our hearts to keep this law.**

Remember that thou keep holy the Sabbath day.
Six days shalt thou labour, and do all that thou hast to do;
but the seventh day is the Sabbath of the Lord thy God.
In it thou shalt do no manner of work,
thou, and thy son, and thy daughter,
thy manservant, and thy maidservant,
thy cattle, and the stranger that is within thy gates.
For in six days the Lord made heaven and earth,
the sea, and all that in them is,
and rested the seventh day:
wherefore the Lord blessed the seventh day, and hallowed it.

All **Lord, have mercy upon us,
and incline our hearts to keep this law.**

Honour thy father and thy mother;
that thy days may be long in the land
    which the Lord thy God giveth thee.

All **Lord, have mercy upon us,
and incline our hearts to keep this law.**

Thou shalt do no murder.

All **Lord, have mercy upon us,
and incline our hearts to keep this law.**

Thou shalt not commit adultery.

All **Lord, have mercy upon us,
and incline our hearts to keep this law.**

Thou shalt not steal.

All **Lord, have mercy upon us,
and incline our hearts to keep this law.**

Thou shalt not bear false witness against thy neighbour.

All **Lord, have mercy upon us,
and incline our hearts to keep this law.**

Thou shalt not covet thy neighbour's house,
thou shalt not covet thy neighbour's wife, nor his servant,
nor his maid, nor his ox, nor his ass, nor anything that is his.

All **Lord, have mercy upon us,
and write all these thy laws in our hearts, we beseech thee.**

Or this Summary of the Law may be said

Our Lord Jesus Christ said:
Hear, O Israel, the Lord our God is one Lord;
and thou shalt love the Lord thy God with all thy heart,
and with all thy soul, and with all thy mind,
and with all thy strength.
This is the first commandment.

And the second is like, namely this:
Thou shalt love thy neighbour as thyself.
There is none other commandment greater than these.
On these two commandments hang all the law and the prophets.

All **Lord, have mercy upon us,
and write all these thy laws in our hearts, we beseech thee.**

Or the Kyrie eleison may be sung or said

Lord, have mercy.

All **Lord, have mercy.**

Lord, have mercy.

All **Christ, have mercy.**

Christ, have mercy.

All **Christ, have mercy.**

Lord, have mercy.

All **Lord, have mercy.**

Lord, have mercy.

(or)

Kyrie, eleison.

All **Kyrie, eleison.**

Kyrie, eleison.

All **Christe, eleison.**

Christe, eleison.

All **Christe, eleison.**

Kyrie, eleison.

All **Kyrie, eleison.**

Kyrie, eleison.

The Collect for the Sovereign may be said

Almighty God, whose kingdom is everlasting, and power infinite: have mercy upon the whole Church; and so rule the heart of thy chosen servant *Elizabeth, our Queen* and Governor, that she (knowing whose minister she is) may above all things seek thy honour and glory: and that we and all her subjects (duly considering whose authority she hath) may faithfully serve, honour and humbly obey her, in thee, and for thee, according to thy blessed word and ordinance; through Jesus Christ our Lord, who with thee and the Holy Ghost liveth and reigneth, ever one God, world without end.

All **Amen.**

The Collect

The minister may say

The Lord be with you
All **and with thy spirit.**
Let us pray.

Then shall be said the Collect of the Day.

Readings

The readings are governed by authorized lectionary provision.

A Lesson from the Old Testament may be read and a psalm may be used.

The reader says

The Lesson is written in the … chapter of …
beginning at the … verse.

At the end

Here endeth the Lesson.

The reader says

The Epistle is written in the … chapter of …
beginning at the … verse.

At the end

Here endeth the Epistle.

Gospel

The reader says

The holy Gospel is written in the … chapter of the Gospel according
to Saint …, beginning at the … verse.

All may respond

All **Glory be to thee, O Lord.**

At the end the reader may say

This is the Gospel of the Lord.

All may respond

All **Praise be to thee, O Christ.**

The Creed

*On Sundays and Principal Holy Days the Nicene Creed is used,
or on occasion the Apostles' Creed or an authorized Affirmation of Faith
may be used.*

All **I believe in one God the Father almighty,
maker of heaven and earth,
and of all things
visible and invisible:**

**And in one Lord Jesus Christ,
the only-begotten Son of God,
begotten of his Father before all worlds,
God of God, Light of Light,
very God of very God,
begotten, not made,
being of one substance with the Father,
by whom all things were made;
who for us men and for our salvation
came down from heaven,
and was incarnate by the Holy Ghost of the Virgin Mary,
and was made man,
and was crucified also for us under Pontius Pilate.
He suffered and was buried,
and the third day he rose again
according to the Scriptures,
and ascended into heaven,
and sitteth on the right hand of the Father.
And he shall come again with glory
to judge both the quick and the dead:
whose kingdom shall have no end.**

**And I believe in the Holy Ghost,
the Lord and giver of life,
who proceedeth from the Father and the Son,
who with the Father and the Son together
is worshipped and glorified,
who spake by the prophets.
And I believe one catholic and apostolic Church.
I acknowledge one baptism for the remission of sins.
And I look for the resurrection of the dead,
and the life of the world to come.
Amen.**

Sermon

Sentence

One of the following or another sentence of Scripture is used

Let your light so shine before men, that they may see your good works, and glorify your Father which is in heaven.   *Matthew 5.16*

Lay not up for yourselves treasures upon earth; where the rust and moth doth corrupt, and where thieves break through and steal: but lay up for yourselves treasures in heaven; where neither rust nor moth doth corrupt, and where thieves do not break through and steal.   *Matthew 6.19*

All things come of thee, and of thine own do we give thee.
1 Chronicles 29.14

Whoso hath this world's goods, and seeth his brother have need, and shutteth up his compassion from him, how dwelleth the love of God in him?   *1 John 3.17*

A hymn may be sung and a collection may be taken.

Intercession

Brief biddings may be given.

Let us pray for the whole state of Christ's Church militant here in earth.

Almighty and ever-living God, who by thy holy apostle hast taught us to make prayers and supplications, and to give thanks, for all men: we humbly beseech thee most mercifully to receive these our prayers, which we offer unto thy divine majesty; beseeching thee to inspire continually the universal Church with the spirit of truth, unity, and concord: and grant, that all they that do confess thy holy name may agree in the truth of thy holy word, and live in unity and godly love.

We beseech thee also to save and defend all Christian kings, princes and governors; and specially thy servant *Elizabeth our Queen*, that under her we may be godly and quietly governed: and grant unto her whole Council, and to all that are put in authority under her, that they may truly and impartially minister justice, to the punishment of wickedness and vice, and to the maintenance of thy true religion and virtue.

Give grace, O heavenly Father, to all bishops, priests and deacons, that they may both by their life and doctrine set forth thy true and lively word, and rightly and duly administer thy holy sacraments: and to all thy people give thy heavenly grace; and specially to this congregation here present; that, with meek heart and due reverence, they may hear and receive thy holy word; truly serving thee in holiness and righteousness all the days of their life.

And we most humbly beseech thee of thy goodness, O Lord, to comfort and succour all them, who in this transitory life are in trouble, sorrow, need, sickness, or any other adversity.

And we also bless thy holy name for all thy servants departed this life in thy faith and fear; beseeching thee to give us grace so to follow their good examples, that with them we may be partakers of thy heavenly kingdom.

Grant this, O Father, for Jesus Christ's sake, our only mediator and advocate.

All **Amen.**

Invitation to Confession

The minister reads the shorter exhortation as follows

Ye that do truly and earnestly repent you of your sins, and are in
love and charity with your neighbours, and intend to lead a new life,
following the commandments of God, and walking from henceforth
in his holy ways: draw near with faith, and take this holy sacrament
to your comfort; and make your humble confession to almighty
God, meekly kneeling upon your knees.

Confession

All   **Almighty God,**
Father of our Lord Jesus Christ,
maker of all things, judge of all men:
we acknowledge and bewail
   our manifold sins and wickedness,
which we, from time to time,
   most grievously have committed,
by thought, word and deed,
against thy divine majesty,
provoking most justly thy wrath and indignation against us.
We do earnestly repent,
and are heartily sorry for these our misdoings;
the remembrance of them is grievous unto us;
the burden of them is intolerable.
Have mercy upon us,
have mercy upon us, most merciful Father;
for thy Son our Lord Jesus Christ's sake,
forgive us all that is past;
and grant that we may ever hereafter
serve and please thee in newness of life,
to the honour and glory of thy name;
through Jesus Christ our Lord.
Amen.

Grant, we beseech thee, merciful Lord,
to thy faithful people pardon and peace,
that they may be cleansed from all their sins,
and serve thee with a quiet mind;
through Jesus Christ our Lord.

All **Amen.**

The Comfortable Words

Hear what comfortable words our Saviour Christ saith unto all that truly turn to him:

Come unto me, all that travail and are heavy laden,
and I will refresh you.   *Matthew 11.28*

So God loved the world, that he gave his only-begotten Son,
to the end that all that believe in him should not perish,
but have everlasting life.   *John 3.16*

Hear also what Saint Paul saith:
This is a true saying, and worthy of all men to be received,
that Christ Jesus came into the world to save sinners.
                    1 Timothy 1.15

Hear also what Saint John saith:
If any man sin, we have an advocate with the Father,
Jesus Christ the righteous;
and he is the propitiation for our sins.   *1 John 2.1*

The following or some other suitable form of thanksgiving is said

All **Almighty God, Father of all mercies,**
we thine unworthy servants
   do give thee most humble and hearty thanks
for all thy goodness and loving-kindness to us, and to all men.
We bless thee for our creation, preservation,
   and all the blessings of this life;
but above all for thine inestimable love
in the redemption of the world by our Lord Jesus Christ,
for the means of grace, and for the hope of glory.
And we beseech thee, give us that due sense of all thy mercies,
that our hearts may be unfeignedly thankful,
and that we shew forth thy praise, not only with our lips,
   but in our lives;
by giving up ourselves to thy service,
and by walking before thee in holiness and righteousness
   all our days;
through Jesus Christ our Lord,
to whom with thee and the Holy Ghost
be all honour and glory, world without end.
Amen.

A hymn may be sung.

At the lectern or minister's stall one of the following shall be read:

Mark 10.32-34, 42-45   *The Son of Man came to give his life.*

Luke 24.30-34   *They recognized him in the breaking of bread.*

John 6.53-58   *My flesh is true food and my blood is true drink.*

Revelation 19.6-9a   *The marriage supper of the Lamb.*

1 Peter 2.21-25   *He bore our sins on the cross.*

Prayer of Humble Access

We do not presume
to come to this thy table, O merciful Lord,
trusting in our own righteousness,
but in thy manifold and great mercies.
We are not worthy
so much as to gather up the crumbs under thy table.
But thou art the same Lord,
whose property is always to have mercy:
grant us therefore, gracious Lord,
so to eat the flesh of thy dear Son Jesus Christ,
and to drink his blood,
that our sinful bodies may be made clean by his body,
and our souls washed through his most precious blood,
and that we may evermore dwell in him, and he in us.

All **Amen.**

Giving of Communion

The minister says

The Church of God, of which we are members, has taken bread and wine and given thanks over them according to our Lord's command. These holy gifts have been brought to us that we too may share in the communion of the body and blood of Christ.

The minister and people receive communion. To each is said

The body of our Lord Jesus Christ, which was given for thee,
preserve thy body and soul unto everlasting life.
Take and eat this in remembrance that Christ died for thee,
and feed on him in thy heart by faith with thanksgiving.

The blood of our Lord Jesus Christ, which was shed for thee,
preserve thy body and soul unto everlasting life.
Drink this in remembrance that Christ's blood was shed for thee,
    and be thankful.

Or, when occasion requires, these words may be said once to each row of communicants, or to a convenient number within each row.

What remains of the consecrated bread and wine which is not required for purposes of communion is consumed now or at the end of the service.

The Lord's Prayer

As our Saviour Christ hath commanded and taught us,
we are bold to say

All **Our Father, which art in heaven,**
hallowed be thy name;
thy kingdom come;
thy will be done,
in earth as it is in heaven.
Give us this day our daily bread.
And forgive us our trespasses,
as we forgive them that trespass against us.
And lead us not into temptation;
but deliver us from evil.
For thine is the kingdom,
the power and the glory,
for ever and ever.
Amen.

Alternatively the Lord's Prayer may be said before the giving of communion.

Silence is kept.

Prayer after Communion

This prayer is said

Almighty and ever-living God, we most heartily thank thee, for that thou dost vouchsafe to feed us, who have duly received these holy mysteries, with the spiritual food of the most precious body and blood of thy Son our Saviour Jesus Christ; and dost assure us thereby of thy favour and goodness towards us; and that we are very members incorporate in the mystical body of thy Son, which is the blessed company of all faithful people; and are also heirs through hope of thy everlasting kingdom, by the merits of the most precious death and passion of thy dear Son. And we most humbly beseech thee, O heavenly Father, so to assist us with thy grace, that we may continue in that holy fellowship, and do all such good works as thou hast prepared for us to walk in; through Jesus Christ our Lord, to whom, with thee and the Holy Ghost, be all honour and glory, world without end.

All **Amen.**

Gloria in Excelsis

All   **Glory be to God on high,
and in earth peace, good will towards men.**

**We praise thee, we bless thee,
we worship thee, we glorify thee,
we give thanks to thee for thy great glory,
O Lord God, heavenly King,
God the Father almighty.**

**O Lord, the only-begotten Son Jesu Christ;
O Lord God, Lamb of God, Son of the Father,
that takest away the sins of the world,
have mercy upon us.
Thou that takest away the sins of the world,
have mercy upon us.
Thou that takest away the sins of the world,
receive our prayer.
Thou that sittest at the right hand of God the Father,
have mercy upon us.**

**For thou only art holy;
thou only art the Lord;
thou only, O Christ,
with the Holy Ghost,
art most high
in the glory of God the Father.
Amen.**

The Grace

The grace of our Lord Jesus Christ,
and the love of God,
and the fellowship of the Holy Ghost,
be with us all evermore.

All   **Amen.**

The minister and people depart.

Public Worship
with
Communion by Extension

Guidelines issued by the House of Bishops

Guidelines issued by
the House of Bishops

1   In making authorized provision for Communion by Extension, the
    House of Bishops has principally in mind the needs of a single cure
    with a number of authorized places of worship, or a group or team
    ministry. In such circumstances worshippers gathered in one of
    the places where Holy Communion has not been celebrated
    may receive communion by extension from a church where Holy
    Communion is celebrated, with a minimal interval of time between
    the services. The provision is intended primarily for Sundays and
    Principal Holy Days, but may be appropriate on other occasions.
    A particular congregation should not come to rely mainly upon
    this means of eucharistic participation, and care should be taken to
    ensure that a celebration of Holy Communion takes place regularly
    in each church concerned.

2   The practice of Communion by Extension as envisaged by the
    authorized service has some affinities with the communion of the
    sick, from elements which have been consecrated at a celebration
    in church. The main differences concern the public nature of
    Communion by Extension, and the consequent need for careful
    attention to the overall shape and content of the service. For this
    reason it is required that the service should be led only by a person
    who has been specifically authorized for this purpose by the bishop.
    Such a person will normally be a deacon, Reader or lay worker
    licensed under Canon E 7, and must wear the appropriate vesture.
    The choice of readings is governed by an authorized lectionary
    provision followed either by a sermon or a suitable devotional
    reading. Those who have been given permission (under the
    provisions of Canon B 12) to assist in the distribution of Holy
    Communion may assist in that way, but the minister who leads
    the service must have a more specific authority from the bishop,
    and be appropriately trained.

3   Communion by Extension should not be regarded as a means of
    introducing a sacramental element into the life of home groups,
    or other parish groups, whether on an occasional or a regular basis.
    The House of Bishops recognizes the value of an occasional
    celebration of Holy Communion in such circumstances, when
    a priest must preside.

4   The service of Communion by Extension has been drawn up to make clear that it is not in itself a celebration of Holy Communion, and yet enables a worshipping community to participate in Holy Communion 'by extension'. When it is introduced to a congregation care should be taken to explain the close relationship between the two services; there is but one celebration of Holy Communion, from which the consecrated elements are brought.

5   The notes which accompany the service make clear that explicit permission must be obtained from the bishop for the use of this rite, and that such permission should relate to specific pastoral circumstances. Such permission will normally be in writing, and will be either for a particular occasion or for a limited duration. The bishop should regularly review the use of this rite in parishes where it is used. Communion by Extension must always be regarded as exceptional and provisional, looking to circumstances when a priest will be available to preside at a celebration of Holy Communion.

6   Communion by Extension will require that special care is given to the conduct of the service, and especially that the consecrated elements are treated in a seemly and dignified manner. Those responsible for a service should ensure that the consecrated elements are adequate to meet the needs of the congregation, and that any consecrated bread and wine which is not required for the purposes of communion is consumed either during or immediately after the service.

7   These guidelines should be read closely with, and be regarded as subordinate to, the notes and rubrics which accompany the authorized rite, which must be observed with care. They are intended to supplement and interpret the notes and rubrics in the service, and the House of Bishops will revise and reissue these guidelines from time to time.

These Guidelines are approved by the House of Bishops from October 2000 until any further resolution of that House.

A Form of Preparation

This form may be used in any of three ways.

It may be used by individuals as part of their preparation for Holy Communion.

It may be used corporately on suitable occasions within Holy Communion where it replaces the sections entitled 'Prayer of Preparation' and 'Prayers of Penitence'.

It may be used as a separate service of preparation. When used in this way, there should be added at the beginning a greeting and at the end the Peace and the Lord's Prayer. Hymns, psalms and other suitable liturgical material may also be included.

Come, Holy Ghost *(Veni creator Spiritus)*

All **Come, Holy Ghost, our souls inspire,
And lighten with celestial fire;
Thou the anointing Spirit art,
Who dost thy sevenfold gifts impart.**

**Thy blessed unction from above
Is comfort, life and fire of love;
Enable with perpetual light
The dullness of our blinded sight.**

**Anoint and cheer our soiled face
With the abundance of thy grace;
Keep far our foes, give peace at home;
Where thou art guide no ill can come.**

**Teach us to know the Father, Son,
And thee, of Both, to be but One;
That through the ages all along
This may be our endless song:**

**Praise to thy eternal merit,
Father, Son and Holy Spirit.
Amen.**

Exhortation

As we gather at the Lord's table we must recall the promises and
warnings given to us in the Scriptures and so examine ourselves and
repent of our sins. We should give thanks to God for his redemption
of the world through his Son Jesus Christ and, as we remember
Christ's death for us and receive the pledge of his love, resolve
to serve him in holiness and righteousness all the days of our life.

The Commandments

Hear the commandments which God has given to his people,
and examine your hearts.

I am the Lord your God: you shall have no other gods but me.

All **Amen. Lord, have mercy.**

You shall not make for yourself any idol.

All **Amen. Lord, have mercy.**

You shall not dishonour the name of the Lord your God.

All **Amen. Lord, have mercy.**

Remember the Sabbath and keep it holy.

All **Amen. Lord, have mercy.**

Honour your father and your mother.

All **Amen. Lord, have mercy.**

You shall not commit murder.

All **Amen. Lord, have mercy.**

You shall not commit adultery.

All **Amen. Lord, have mercy.**

You shall not steal.

All **Amen. Lord, have mercy.**

You shall not bear false witness against your neighbour.

All **Amen. Lord, have mercy.**

You shall not covet anything which belongs to your neighbour.

All **Amen. Lord, have mercy upon us**
     and write all these your laws in our hearts.

Or one of the forms of the Commandments in the Supplementary Texts on pages 269–271 of Common Worship: Services and Prayers for the Church of England *may be used.*

Or, in place of the Commandments, one of these texts may be used.

Summary of the Law

Our Lord Jesus Christ said:
The first commandment is this:
'Hear, O Israel, the Lord our God is the only Lord.
You shall love the Lord your God with all your heart,
with all your soul, with all your mind,
and with all your strength.'

The second is this: 'Love your neighbour as yourself.'
There is no other commandment greater than these.
On these two commandments hang all the law and the prophets.

All **Amen. Lord, have mercy**.

(or)

The Comfortable Words

Hear the words of comfort our Saviour Christ says
to all who truly turn to him:

Come to me, all who labour and are heavy laden,
and I will give you rest.   *Matthew 11.28*

God so loved the world that he gave his only-begotten Son,
that whoever believes in him should not perish
but have eternal life.   *John 3.16*

Hear what Saint Paul says:
This saying is true, and worthy of full acceptance,
that Christ Jesus came into the world to save sinners. *1 Timothy 1.15*

Hear what Saint John says:
If anyone sins, we have an advocate with the Father,
Jesus Christ the righteous;
and he is the propitiation for our sins.   *1 John 2.1, 2*

(or)

The Beatitudes

Let us hear our Lord's blessing on those who follow him.

Blessed are the poor in spirit,
for theirs is the kingdom of heaven.

Blessed are those who mourn,
for they shall be comforted.

Blessed are the meek,
for they shall inherit the earth.

Blessed are those who hunger and thirst after righteousness,
for they shall be satisfied.

Blessed are the merciful,
for they shall obtain mercy.

Blessed are the pure in heart,
for they shall see God.

Blessed are the peacemakers,
for they shall be called children of God.

Blessed are those who suffer persecution for righteousness' sake,
for theirs is the kingdom of heaven.

Silence for Reflection

Confession

All **Father eternal, giver of light and grace,**
we have sinned against you and against our neighbour,
in what we have thought,
in what we have said and done,
through ignorance, through weakness,
through our own deliberate fault.
We have wounded your love
and marred your image in us.
We are sorry and ashamed
and repent of all our sins.
For the sake of your Son Jesus Christ,
who died for us,
forgive us all that is past
and lead us out from darkness
to walk as children of light.
Amen.

Or another authorized confession may be used.

Absolution

Almighty God, our heavenly Father,
who in his great mercy
has promised forgiveness of sins
to all those who with heartfelt repentance and true faith
    turn to him:
have mercy on us;
pardon and deliver us from all our sins;
confirm and strengthen us in all goodness;
and bring us to everlasting life;
through Jesus Christ our Lord.

All **Amen.**

General Rules for Regulating Authorized Forms of Service

1   Any reference in authorized provision to the use of hymns shall be construed as including the use of texts described as songs, chants, canticles.

2   If occasion requires, hymns may be sung at points other than those indicated in particular forms of service. Silence may be kept at points other than those indicated in particular forms of service.

3   Where rubrics indicate that a text is to be 'said' this must be understood to include 'or sung' and vice versa.

4   Where parts of a service make use of well-known and traditional texts, other translations or versions, particularly when used in musical compositions, may be used.

5   Local custom may be established and followed in respect of posture but regard should be had to indications in Notes attached to authorized forms of service that a particular posture is appropriate for some parts of that form of service.

6   On any occasion when the text of an alternative service authorized under the provisions of Canon B 2 provides for the Lord's Prayer to be said or sung, it may be used in the form included in *The Book of Common Prayer* or in either of the two other forms included in services in *Common Worship*. The further text included in Prayers for Various Occasions in *Common Worship: Services and Prayers for the Church of England* (page 106) may be used on suitable occasions.

7   Normally on any occasion only one Collect is used.

8   At Baptisms, Confirmations, Ordinations and Marriages which take place on Principal Feasts, other Principal Holy Days and on Sundays of Advent, Lent and Easter, within the Celebration of the Holy Communion, the Readings of the day are used and the Collect of the Day is said, unless the bishop directs otherwise.

9   The Collects and Lectionary in *Common Worship* may, optionally, be used in conjunction with the days included in the Calendar of *The Book of Common Prayer*, notwithstanding any difference in the title or name of a Sunday, Holy Day or other observance included in both Calendars.

Authorization

The texts of services contained in this booklet are authorized pursuant to Canon B 2 of the Canons of the Church of England for use until further resolution of the General Synod.

The Guidelines are approved by the House of Bishops from October 2000 until any further resolution of that House.

Acknowledgements

The publisher gratefully acknowledges permission to reproduce copyright material in this book.

Published sources include the following:

The English Language Liturgical Consultation: English translation of Gloria in excelsis, Kyrie eleison, the Lord's Prayer and the Nicene Creed prepared by the English Language Liturgical Consultation, based on (or excerpted from) *Praying Together* © ELLC 1988.

The Archbishops' Council of the Church of England: *The Prayer Book as Proposed in 1928*, which is copyright © The Archbishops' Council of the Church of England.

Cambridge University Press: Extracts (and adapted extracts) from *The Book of Common Prayer*, the rights in which are vested in the Crown, are reproduced by permission of the Crown's Patentee, Cambridge University Press.